FREDA KELSALL

A & C Black in association with ❤Yorkshire Television

Contents

Kelsall, Freda
    How we used to live.
    1. Great Britain—Social life and customs
    —20th century
    I. Title
    941.083   DA566.4
    ISBN 0-7136-2623-2

Published by A & C Black (Publishers) Limited
35 Bedford Row, London WC1R 4JH

First published 1985
© 1985 (text) Freda Kelsall

Reprinted 1985, 1987

ISBN 0-7136-2623-2

Filmset by Method Limited, Epping, Essex
Printed in Hong Kong for Imago Publishing Limited

Acknowledgements

Historical advisor, Norman Longmate.

Pictures by Barnaby's Picture Library pages 3, 12,
20 (bottom), 21 (bottom), 32 (bottom), 33 (top), 43 (top), 44;
BBC Hulton Picture Library pages 4, 6, 7 (bottom),
8 (bottom), 9, 10, 14, 15, 18, 19, 21 (left), 22, 23 (bottom
right), 31 (top right, bottom), 33 (bottom), 34, 35, 37
(bottom), 38, 39, 40 (top right), 42; C I Browne page 17
(top); Tony Garrett map page 23; Imperial War Museum
pages 23 (bottom left), 24 (top left, bottom), 26, 27, 28, 29,
30; Freda Kelsall page 7 (top right); Mary Evans Picture
Library pages 11, 13, 17 (bottom), 20 (top), 25, 31 (middle
left), 32 (top), 36, 37 (top right and left), 40 (top left), 41
(left); John Topham Picture Library pages 7 (top left), 8
(top), 16, 24 (top right), 40 (bottom), 41 (right), 43 (bottom),
45, 47; page 5 © Yorkshire Television. D. Scott-Stewart tints
for cover photograph.

How We Used to Live is a Yorkshire Television production.
Executive producer, Chris Jelley; Producer, Ian Fell;
Director, Carol Wilks.

▶ A house in Amersham, decorated to celebrate Edward
VII's coronation.

A new century

In January 1901 Queen Victoria died. To many British people, this was the beginning of a new age. What would the twentieth century bring?

There were exciting hints of change. That year, wireless signals had crossed the Atlantic for the first time and, in 1902, an airship was seen crossing London.

At the end of Queen Victoria's reign, Britain was the richest country in the world. Victoria had ruled over a huge Empire and Britain controlled a large part of the world's trade. British ships travelled all over the globe, taking British goods and bringing back cheap grain, frozen meat and many other cargoes.

Middle-class families, who made their wealth from trade and industry, lived in large houses with several servants to look after them. Most people took it for granted that a factory owner would live a very different life from the people he employed. His workers earned very low wages for long hours, often in dangerous, unhealthy conditions.

Those who were too old or ill to work, or who couldn't find a job, had very little help from the rest of society.

The new century brought hints of change here, too. People were beginning to think that 'Labour' should be better represented in Parliament and that the nation's wealth should be shared more fairly.

When Edward VII came to the throne, people looked forward to a time of peace, wealth and progress. But few people even dreamed of the changes which the next twenty-five years would bring.

◄ An invitation to celebrate the coronation of Edward VII. The dinner never took place because the King had appendicitis. His coronation was postponed and the expensive food was distributed to the poor of London's East End.

1. Home and family, 1902

At home

During Victoria's reign, many new factories and mills had been built. Thousands of people had flocked to the towns to look for jobs. They had been housed as quickly and cheaply as possible, in narrow streets of terraced houses.

Most terraced houses were 'two-up-two-down', with two rooms on the ground floor and two on the first floor. There wasn't much space for a large family. As well as the four main rooms the family might have an attic, a basement, and a scullery where the washing was done.

Many working-class families were still living in these houses when Victoria died and Edward VII was crowned. In some areas, the houses had been 'modernised'. They might have a cold tap in the kitchen or scullery, so that families didn't have to fetch water in buckets from a stand pipe (tap) in the street. In towns, houses would have gas lighting, usually for the downstairs rooms only. Some families had an outside toilet built next to the coalstore in the yard.

The kitchen was usually the warmest room in the house. It was heated by a coal fire. On top of the fire was a hob (hot-plate) for boiling kettles and heating irons. The fire was also used to heat the oven for cooking.

Hot water for washing often had to be heated on the fire, too. Clothes were washed in a big tub, called a 'copper', which was built into the scullery. The clothes had to be boiled in water and soapflakes and pounded until they were clean. Then they were hung out to dry on washing lines across the street. Unfortunately, the air was so smoky from all the chimneys on factories and people's houses, that the family washing often got covered in soot and dirt before it was dry.

You can still see the houses where Edwardian working-class families lived. Many of them have now been modernised into comfortable small homes. Central heating, bathrooms and modern kitchens have made quite a difference.

Larger houses, which were occupied by wealthy Edwardians, are less often used as family homes today. You may have seen some which have been divided into flats or offices. They often had more than eight rooms, including a drawing room, morning room, dining room and attic bedrooms for the servants.

The family would have several servants to look after their big house. The household could include a nanny, butler, cook, parlourmaid, footman, gardener, groom and several others, all working long hours.

Wealthy Edwardians often had a telephone and electric light. Their houses were usually heated by coal fires in every room. The servants had to carry coal upstairs and refill the coal scuttles several times a day. They would also make sure that the fires were lit in the bedrooms every evening, and in the dining rooms for meal times. Town houses might have gas fires, and a very few homes had central heating radiators from coke-fired boilers in their cellars.

▼ The Selby family having tea in the kitchen, from the Yorkshire Television series 'How We Used to Live' (1902-1926). The kitchen was the main room in the house and was often overcrowded.

▲ Miss Holroyd and the chapel minister having tea in the parlour. The family would eat their main meals in the dining room. Food was prepared by the servants in the kitchen and then brought upstairs.

Many of these large houses were richly furnished and decorated. Victorian furniture had mainly been heavy and dark. But a Victorian artist, called William Morris, had helped to change people's ideas about decoration. Morris had designed his own furniture, wallpaper and carpets. Partly because of his influence, Edwardian houses became lighter and airier.

The old, dark Victorian furniture was covered with flowered chintz, and wood was enamelled pale cream, or white. A child's room might have had high-backed chairs with rush seats, called 'Cottage' furniture, from Heal and Co.

Some museums show what houses of this period looked like inside. They are well worth a visit if there is one near you.

2. Chapel on Sunday, 1903

Chapel and the Temperance Movement

Victorians had been very strict about keeping Sunday as a day of rest. No shops or factories were open. People would dress up in their best clothes and go to church. Roman Catholics went to Mass. The Church of England held services in parish churches. Nonconformists, such as Methodists, Baptists and Congregationalists, worshipped in chapels.

Churches and chapels were not only places of worship. In Victorian times there were no free hospitals or schools and no old-age pensions or unemployment benefit. The churches and chapels helped to provide schools for people who could not afford expensive education. They also raised money for hospitals and charities.

By 1902, the Church was becoming less important. The government started to provide schools for children up to the age of twelve. Fewer young men wanted to be clergymen. They went into other careers, such as business, law or the civil service. Country churches were left half empty as more and more people moved into the towns.

A survey for the 'Daily News' showed that from 1902-1903 only two in every eleven adults regularly attended any place of worship in London.

This was not true all over the country. In many of the northern industrial towns and in Welsh mining villages, the Nonconformist chapels were an important part of people's day to day lives. As well as Sunday School, the chapels held 'Sunday afternoons' with music and talks on the social reforms needed to help the poor. They were also places to discuss political subjects such as the Trade Unions and the new Labour Movement.

Many Chapel goers were also members of the Temperance Movement. They believed that drinking alcohol was wrong. Unlike members of the Church of England, who felt that there was no harm in moderate drinking, many Chapel members thought that even one drink could lead to bad habits and drunkenness.

This was partly because the chapels were based in towns built around factories and mills. Here, people worked hard for long hours. There wasn't much room or comfort at home. Public houses were open longer hours than they are today.

▲ Lunchtime on a children's outing. Treats and excursions were organised by Sunday Schools and the 'Band of Hope'.

Many men spent their free time in public houses to forget their troubles at work and at home. Sometimes, this meant that there wasn't enough money to pay the rent or buy food. Drunkards and their families could end up in prison, or the workhouse.

The chapels encouraged people, especially Sunday School children, to join 'The Band of Hope' and sign a pledge saying that they would never drink alcohol.

Chapel members organised entertainments to keep people away from the public houses. There were concerts and magic lantern shows for members, and lectures, parties and outings. Instead of alcohol, buns, lemonade and ginger beer would be served.

▲ In this Lancashire Temperance bar, only soft drinks were sold. Summer drinks for a penny included non-alcoholic fruit-wine and ginger-beer.

◄ Many children signed a 'pledge card' like this one and promised never to drink or smoke.

▼ The Salvation Army tried to provide food, shelter and 'honest' work for the poor. It was started in Victorian times by William Booth, a Methodist who went to preach in the East End of London. This picture shows a stall of goods made by 'inebriates' (drunkards) – members of the Salvation Army did not drink or smoke.

Most people, except for domestic servants and shop assistants, had some free time in the evenings and at weekends. Even shop assistants had Sundays free and, from 1911, they also had a regular half-day holiday during the week. Domestic servants had very little time off, but families who believed in 'keeping the Sabbath' made do with a cold Sunday dinner, and let their cooks and housemaids go out.

Football matches drew large crowds on Saturday afternoons. Factories and collieries started up their own brass bands and choirs. As fewer people went to church, museums and art galleries were allowed to open on Sundays.

For evening entertainment, the music halls would soon be competing with Bioscopes. These were early cinemas, showing silent moving pictures. In 1904, Britain's first regular cinema 'The Daily Bioscope' opened in London. It offered a fifty-minute programme for 3d (less than 2p) or 6d (2½p).

Travelling about town, to a football match or the Bioscope, was made easier by the new electric trams. These ran along tram-lines in the street and were connected to electric cables overhead.

◀ A poster advertising trips to the seaside.

3. Bank Holiday, 1905

Holidays and outings

If you look at Edwardian photographs or diaries, you might begin to think that people spent all their time at picnics and outings, or fashionable dinners.

You might also find photographs of working people in their best clothes, enjoying a day off. They would often have special 'holiday photographs' taken. For the rest of the year they worked fifty-two hours a week. They didn't have long holidays on full pay as we do today.

This meant that a Bank Holiday was a rare treat. The railway companies laid on special Excursion trains from industrial towns to seaside resorts. Travelling fairs and circuses arrived, there were sporting events, and bands gave concerts in public parks. If this sounds a bit too energetic, remember that a lot of fun had to be packed into a very short time.

In London, there was also the 'Tuppenny Tube', which opened in 1900. The very first 'underground' had been opened in 1863. Its trains were powered by steam and were very dirty and noisy. The 'Tuppenny Tube' trains were powered by electricity, and looked much more like the underground trains we use today. Their most popular feature was the standard fare. For 2d, a passenger could travel for any distance along the line.

Above ground, London's streets were chaotic. Horse-drawn cabs and carriages competed for space with bicycles, trams and the new motor-buses. Only the very rich could afford motor cars, so cheap public transport was very important. It allowed ordinary people to travel much more quickly and to visit places and do things which they could never have done before.

▲ London's first electric tram, 1903. The Prince of Wales (later King George V) performed the opening ceremony. The use of electricity helped to improve public transport, but many vehicles, like the fire engine in this picture, were still pulled by horses.

MISS PAULINE CHASE   MISS ADRIENNE AUGARDE
MISS NINA SEVENING   MISS CARRIE MOORE

◄ Motoring was still a novelty, the hobby of a few rich people. Motor cars were noisy and churned up clouds of dust. Their design earned them the name 'horseless carriages'. It would be some years before the internal combustion engine became more popular than the horse.

◄ Building sandcastles at Bamburgh. Even on the beach, girls wore big hats and kept their stockings on unless they were paddling.

▼ From 'Round about a pound a week' by Maude Pember Reeves, 1913.

Budget of the family of a railway-carriage washer, who earned 21 shillings (£1.10p) for a seven-day week in 1911. He had a wife and three children.

	s – d
Rent	7 – 0
Clothing club (2 weeks)	1 – 2
Burial insurance (2 weeks)	1 – 6
Coal and wood	1 – 7
Coke	0 – 3
Gas	0 – 10
Soap, soda	0 – 5
Matches	0 – 1
Blacklead, blacking	0 – 1
	12 – 11

Left over for food: 8 – 1

11 loaves	2 – 7
1 quartern flour	0 – 5½
Meat	1 – 10
Potatoes and greens	0 – 9½
½lb butter	0 – 6
1lb jam	0 – 3
6 ozs tea	0 – 6
2lb sugar	0 – 4
1 tin milk	0 – 4
Cocoa	0 – 4
Suet	0 – 2
	8 – 1

4. Vote for changes, 1906
The general election

As more people learned to read, bought the newspapers and travelled to other parts of the country, ordinary working people began to know more about politics.

Men from all walks of life had the right to vote on who should represent them in Parliament. The two main political parties, Conservatives and Liberals, were talked about in pubs and factories, as well as in middle-class villas and stately homes.

In 1905, the Conservatives were in power. But who would form the next government? The main arguments were about the price of food. Many foods imported from abroad were cheaper than foods produced in Britain. People brought frozen meat from Argentina because it was half the price of British meat.

Some Conservatives in Parliament argued that many people would lose their jobs if no-one bought British goods. They wanted to put a tax on all goods which did not come from the British Empire. But the new taxes would mean that bread and many other foods would become more expensive.

The Liberal party were against taxing imported goods. They offered voters a choice between 'the big loaf and the little loaf'.

Many people in Britain already found it difficult to buy the food they needed. They relied mainly on cheap foods, like bread. Charles Booth and Seebohm Rowntree had made a study of people's wages and housekeeping budgets. They showed that over a quarter of the population lived 'below the poverty line'. This meant that they could not afford bare necessities such as food and warm clothing. For these families, the price of food was very important indeed.

The general election was held over several weeks, and results were made known gradually. Magic lanterns were used to project lists of names and voting figures on to large screens in public places.

As the excitement mounted, it became clear that the Liberals would have an astonishing overall majority. The Conservatives lost heavily. The Labour party won twenty-nine seats in the House of Commons and Labour policies were supported by many other M.P.s. How would this new government use its unexpected measure of power?

▲ Grocers like this one were the beginnings of today's supermarkets. Groups of shops bought food in bulk so that they could keep prices down. Much of the food was imported.

▶ This Liberal poster aims to show the danger of Tariff Reform, the Conservative policy to tax imported goods.

Pensions and the budget

Two years after the election the Liberals had a new leader, Herbert Asquith, and a new Chancellor of the Exchequer, David Lloyd George.

On New Year's Day 1909, the government introduced a new scheme – old age pensions. For the first time, the state would give a regular income to elderly people.

Before then, the elderly poor did not have much to look forward to. They expected to work until they were too ill or frail to go on. Very few people on low wages could save for their old age. They depended on sons and daughters, who were often struggling to feed large families of their own.

Elderly people who were not supported by their families often had to go to the workhouse. These gaunt grim buildings were left over from Victorian times. The harsh conditions and disgrace of the workhouse filled old people with dread.

Then came 'The Lloyd George', the five shillings (25p) a week (or seven and sixpence for a married couple) which could make all the difference. It was too small a sum to live on, but with just a few pounds in savings and perhaps a couple of shillings a week from grown-up children, elderly people could avoid poverty and the workhouse. They could retire at the age of seventy and keep their self-respect.

The pensioners collected their money from the Post Office. In the early days of the scheme, some pensioners gave the Post Office clerks small gifts to express their gratitude – almost as if the clerks were giving out their own money.

The money for pensions came out of taxes on the rich. Lloyd George increased the amount of money which people had to pay for death duties on estates. He also increased income tax, introduced a new super-tax, and land value duties to be paid whenever land changed hands.

The new taxes on the rich, in what came to be called the 'People's Budget', caused a sensation. But the amounts taken were very small compared to the taxes we pay today.

The government also needed money from taxes to help reorganise the army and the navy. The Boer War had shown that the army was not as strong as it should have been. Germany had been building up her navy and Britain was lagging behind. R.B. Haldane, the Secretary of State for War, was given the job of reorganising the army and Sir John Fisher was to help build up the navy.

The 'People's Budget' also increased the tax on alcoholic drinks and set up a fund to improve Britain's roads. It raised the money for roads by taxing petrol and motor car licences.

Nowadays we expect to pay all these taxes, but they caused outrage at the time. Although the House of Commons passed the new taxes, the House of Lords would fight against them.

▼ Almshouses in Thaxted, Essex. Charitable organisations helped the elderly poor by providing almshouses, small homes paid for by voluntary donations.

▲ This picture of the Marylebone workhouse shows what conditions could be like for old people before they had pensions to make their savings last longer. Men and women were housed separately, which often meant that elderly couples who had spent most of their lives together were parted in old age.

▶ Many elderly people still lived in Victorian slums like these back-to-back houses in Staithes, Yorkshire. When they became too old to work and couldn't pay the rent, they might be sent to the workhouse.

6. Out of work, 1910

Labour exchanges and the 'Dole'

In 1910, there was no unemployment benefit. People who lost their jobs had no money coming in at all, so they needed to find a new job quickly. The 'People's Budget' included a plan to help people find new jobs.

The government set aside £100 000 to start a national system of Labour Exchanges, with a central headquarters in London. A man who was looking for work could go to a Labour Exchange in his own area and find out about job vacancies near his home, or new openings in other parts of the country.

Some Trade Unionists were against the new scheme. They were afraid that employers might hire 'blackleg' labour from the new Exchanges to replace workers who were on strike.

Other people welcomed the scheme, as it also helped to start a plan for unemployment insurance. This was another idea to help people who were out of work.

While someone had a job, he would pay a small amount out of his wages, to which his employer and the government added more. This would be an insurance against being out of work. If he did lose his job, the Government would give him a small amount of money every week (unemployment benefit) while he tried to find work. The Labour Exchange would help him to find a job. The new unemployment benefit soon came to be called the 'Dole'. It was one of the first steps towards the welfare state as we know it today.

There were fierce struggles in Parliament before any of the new schemes could be introduced. The House of Lords voted against the new taxation and the 'People's Budget'.

▼ A 'Hunger march', 1908.

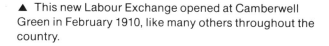

▲ This new Labour Exchange opened at Camberwell Green in February 1910, like many others throughout the country.

Asquith, the Prime Minister, called another election to prove that the voters were in favour of the Budget. He won the election and put forward a new bill which would stop the House of Lords from ever again rejecting the Budget.

Asquith had a daring plan to get the new bill passed by the House of Lords. He was going to ask the King to appoint 250 new peers to the House of Lords – all men who would vote in favour of the new bill. But in the middle of the crisis, on 6 May 1910, Edward VII died.

Edward had reigned for less than ten years, but there had been many important changes while he was on the throne. The old accepted ideas about social class were beginning to be challenged. Edward was succeeded by his son, King George V, and eventually the House of Lords had to accept the 'People's Budget'.

THE DAWN OF HOPE.

Mr. LLOYD GEORGE'S National Health Insurance Bill provides for the insurance of the Worker in case of Sickness.

Support the Liberal Government
in their policy of
SOCIAL REFORM.

▲ People who joined the National Insurance scheme would get a small amount of money every week while they were ill, or out of work. They could also be treated by a 'panel' doctor free of charge.

Working in the town and country

The census of 1911 shows that for the first time in fifty years, the number of farm labourers was rising. This means that some people must have moved from the towns back to the farms and villages.

Farming methods were changing. British farmers could not compete with cheap grain and meat imported from abroad. They produced less wheat and started to grow more fruit and vegetables. Dairying, poultry and egg production also became more popular

Agricultural machines were available, but not many farmers used them. The first efficient tractor with an internal combustion engine had been invented in 1902, but horses were still used to pull the ploughs. Barn machinery, such as threshing machines, could save hours of work. But for a long time farmers wouldn't use them. They were worried that the fuel for the machines might start fires.

Villages didn't have many of the services and amenities which town dwellers were used to. The carrier's cart called once or twice a week bringing oil for the lamps, newspapers, tinned foods and goods which couldn't be produced locally. Postmen delivered the letters by bicycle. There was very little public transport. Most people went about on foot.

Farm labourers were often given a small house to live in as part of their wages. But their employers didn't always look after the houses properly. Roofs leaked and rotten window-frames rattled in winter.

There was no gas or electricity laid on to small villages, and no mains water or sewerage. Wood or peat was burnt on the fire, and oil lamps and candles were used during the long winter evenings. Water was carried from the well or the village pump. These were icy in winter and sometimes dried up during a dry summer.

Farm labourers were paid less than workers in towns and industry. Because they lived in small groups, cut off from each other, it was difficult for them to organise a powerful Union.

In industrial areas, the Trade Unions had become more active and powerful than ever before. Many Union members gave money to support the Labour party. But a new movement in the Trade Unions believed that trying to change things inside Parliament was not enough. Between 1910 and 1912, millions of men went on strike for better wages and conditions. Some of the strikes and disputes led to riots and the army was called in.

In 1910, miners in South Wales were on strike for ten months, and a man was killed in riots at Tonypandy. Churchill, as Home Secretary, reluctantly sent troops and men from the Metropolitan police to help the local Chief Constable keep order.

In 1911, seamen, dockers and railwaymen were on strike. At Liverpool, two men were killed in a clash between troops and rioters. Two more were killed at Llanelly, when soldiers opened fire on looters. Meanwhile, food for town-dwellers rotted in the heat at docks and railway-yards.

Some improvements were made. For instance, the Port of London Authority granted 7d instead of 6d an hour to dockers, and miners were given minimum wage agreements. But these improvements did not include farm labourers. Their wages rose by 9% from the beginning of the century, but were still below average.

▲ Most jobs on the farm were still done by hand and involved the whole family, even the whole village at certain times of the year. Haymaking and harvest kept everyone busy, and were usually followed by a celebration or 'Harvest home'. The photograph shows villagers of Draycott in Gloucestershire.

▼ An artist's painting of a country cottage in the snow. It looks peaceful and charming, but with only a wood fire for heating, the cottage would have been very draughty and bitterly cold in winter.

▲ Gradually, farm work was becoming mechanised. This Ivel Agricultural Motor Hauler, or plough, was available from 1903.

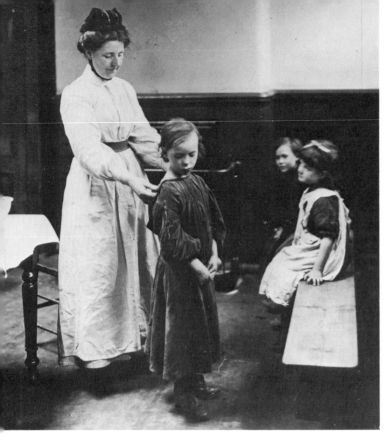

▲ A school medical inspection. Children would be examined for 'nits' (head-lice) and skin-rashes. Their eyes and ears would be tested. Many ailments were caused by poor diet and damp housing. Except for recommending free school meals, the doctors couldn't do much to help.

▼ Exercise in the school yard, 1908. Physical fitness was encouraged by lessons in Swedish drill, a new subject on the time-table in many girls' schools.

8. The Children's Charter, 1912

Conditions for children

At the beginning of this century, few people 'planned' how many children they would have. New babies were sometimes unwelcome in homes which were already overcrowded. Many children died young. People with little money and large families had to bring up their children as best they could. They didn't get much help from the state.

'Elementary' education was free. Children had to go to school until they were twelve years old and had passed the 'standards' of reading, writing and arithmetic. Even if they didn't pass the standards, they left Elementary school at fourteen.

In 1902, the government started to make plans for free secondary schools. It also gave grants to Grammar schools, on condition that a quarter of the pupils should have free places. This meant that children could win scholarships and go to Grammar schools even if their parents could not afford the fees.

Not all the children who won free places were able to take them. If there were younger brothers and sisters, older children were often expected to go to work and bring home wages to help the family budget.

Children could start earning a living at twelve years old. Girls could go into domestic service. They would have their keep provided by employers, which saved on food at home. For boys, there were low-paid 'live-in' jobs as apprentices or shop assistants.

Factories employed 'half-timers', children who went to work for half the day and went to school in the afternoons. Many of these children started work at 6.30 in the morning and fell asleep over their desks at school. Laws were passed to prevent cruelty and control the employment of children. But many parents tried to break the laws, especially in the country where it was hard to check how many hours a child worked.

Children were not only expected to work like adults. If they broke the law, they were treated just like adults. They could be tried in a police court and sent to prison.

The Children's Act of 1908 was known for a long time as 'The Children's Charter'. It made wide changes in the treatment of children who broke the law. Juvenile offenders would now have their cases heard in private, instead of a police court. They could be sent to reformatories, or industrial schools instead of adult prisons. This was to stop them from meeting adult criminals, and to teach them skills which might help them to earn an honest living.

The Probation Act of 1907 meant that children did not have to be punished for small offences and allowed a magistrate to take the age of the child into account. Responsible members of the community were appointed to help look after children who had broken the law, and to make sure that they behaved properly. N.S.P.C.C. officers and Sunday school teachers often volunteered to do this.

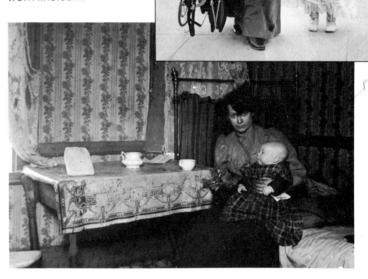

▶ Mothers and children: a middle-class woman (1910) takes her baby for a walk, with a new Sturgis folding baby-carriage in case the toddler gets tired. But in the slums, a poor woman (1912) can hardly afford to feed her baby. Their home is furnished with torn curtains and worn linoleum.

People were beginning to be more concerned about the physical health of children. The Children's Charter banned juvenile smoking. In 1906, local authorities had started to provide free school meals for children who needed them. School medical inspections were introduced, and games and physical training were added to the school time-table.

For younger children, Rachel and Margaret McMillan started mother-and-infant welfare clinics and open air nurseries.

It was a time when the state began to see that it should help parents to look after their children.

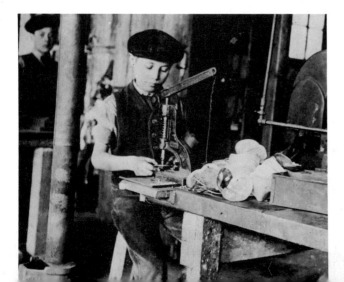

◀ Many boys became apprentices so that they could learn a trade. They were paid very low wages. The new plans for secondary education included places for young men to learn technical skills.

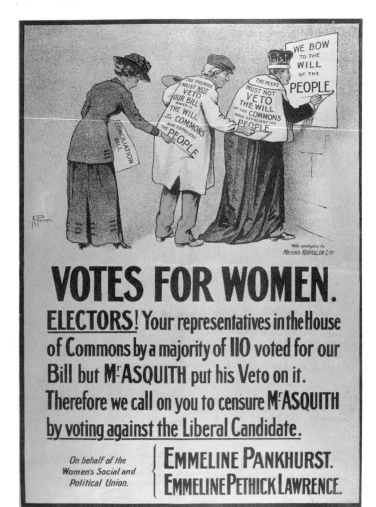

A A W.S.P.U. poster urging people to vote against Liberals. When this had no effect, they tried more violent tactics – in 1913, bombs were set to explode outside Lloyd George's house. Luckily, there was little damage, but another suffragette bomb blew out a stained-glass window at St John's Church, Westminster, just after evening service.

9. The right to vote, 1913

Women's right to vote

During the nineteenth century, many working-class women had jobs in mills and factories, or as domestic servants. Their families needed the money which they earned. But middle-class women were usually expected to stay at home and look after their households.

In the early years of the twentieth century, this was beginning to change. Middle-class women were struggling to enter the professions on equal terms with men. Some succeeded. Elizabeth Garrett Anderson became a qualified doctor and, in 1908, was England's first woman Mayor. The first woman magistrate, Emily Dawson, was appointed in 1913.

Although a woman could qualify as a doctor, she was not allowed to be a member of Parliament, or even vote in elections. In 1903, the Women's Social and Political Union was formed to press for women's right to vote. Led by Mrs Emmeline Pankhurst, the movement began to raise questions at public meetings and organise petitions and demonstrations.

▼ Cheering crowds greet Mrs Pethick-Lawrence after her release from prison. She disagreed with the use of violence and damage to property.

▼ The cause united middle-class and working-class women. By 1912, when this woman took her placard to Westminster, the suffragettes had a bad reputation. But many thousands of women continued to demonstrate without breaking the law.

VOTES FOR WOMEN

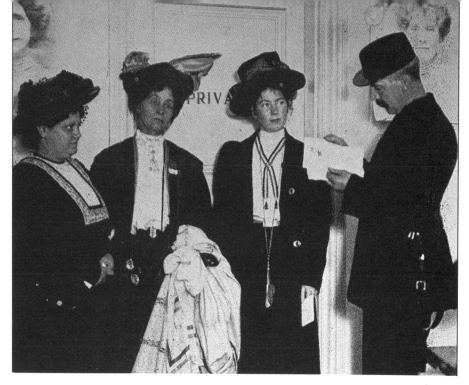

▲ Three leading suffragettes, Mrs Drummond, Mrs Pankhurst and her daughter, Christabel, being questioned by a police inspector. They knew that their activities would lead to prison sentences.

Some men supported the movement, such as Keir Hardie a member of the Labour Party. The Liberal government also took a few steps in the right direction. They passed the Qualification of Women Act (1907), which allowed women to sit on local councils and become Mayors. But many people thought that women should stay at home and keep out of politics. The 'suffragettes', as the women of the W.S.P.U. were called, began to be impatient with such slow progress.

Suffragettes started to disrupt political meetings by shouting at Liberal speakers. They concentrated on Liberals because they had the most seats in Parliament and the power to pass a law giving women the right to vote.

Police were called to remove the suffragettes from meetings. The women fought back by chaining themselves to fixtures like railings. Many women were sent to court and fined. People thought that this would make the suffragettes behave themselves, but it didn't. They refused to pay the fines and were sent to prison.

As a protest the suffragettes refused to eat while they were in prison. The prison officers tried to stop the hunger-strikes by force-feeding their prisoners. Tubes were pushed into the women's stomachs, through the mouth or nose and food was pumped into them against their will. It amounted to torture, as the pain and rough handling could injure the women permanently.

Force-feeding only made the suffragettes more angry and led to violent demonstrations. In 1913, the 'Cat and Mouse Act' was passed. A suffragette could go on hunger-strike in prison, but would be released when she became too weak. Once her health had improved, she could be put back in prison to complete her sentence.

From July 1912, Mrs Pankhurst's daughter, Christabel, started a new and more violent campaign. Women set fire to buildings, planted bombs, cut telephone wires and slashed valuable pictures.

Other suffragette organisations, such as The National Union of Suffrage Societies, did not agree with these new methods. They preferred to campaign by holding peaceful meetings and demonstrations. But soon, the beginning of the First World War would stop all the suffragettes' demonstrations. It would also show that women could do 'men's work' and deserved the vote.

Britain at war

Since the end of the Boer War in South Africa, Britain had been at peace. There had been some fighting in Europe, but few people thought that this would affect Britain.

On 29 June 1914 the newspapers mentioned that the heir to the throne of Austria had been murdered. Many people soon forgot the story. Everyone was looking forward to the August Bank Holiday. But Parliament knew that the situation was serious.

For years, Germany had felt surrounded by rival powers and had been planning to take more territory by force when the right time came. Germany had a huge well-trained army, a strong navy and enough money to put them into action. The murder of the Austrian Archduke was a good excuse for the Kaiser to put the German army and navy to the test.

German troops planned to march through Holland, Luxembourg and Belgium and then invade France. The attack, it was thought, would take six weeks. After this, Germany could join forces with Austria against the Russians.

Britain could not stay out of the war for long. Under a Treaty of 1839, Britain had promised to protect Belgium. German troops marched into Belgium on 4 August 1914, and Britain had to declare war.

Most people thought that the war would be over by Christmas. Young men all over the country wanted to join up and fight. Many of them were too young to join the army and pretended to be eighteen years old rather than miss the adventure.

The British Expeditionary Force crossed the Channel taking 53 000 horses. They expected a fast-moving battle. But by late autumn, people realised that this war was going to be different from any other.

British, French and Belgian soldiers fought together as allies. They dug themselves into lines of trenches to stop the Germans from advancing any further. These lines of trenches came to be called the Western Front. Attackers and defenders bombarded each other, turning the countryside into endless acres of barbed wire and mud.

The British War Minister, Lord Kitchener, called for a new army of 100 000 volunteers. Before the war was over, 702 410 British men would lose their lives, over 500 000 of them killed on the Western Front. These figures don't include the one and a half million seriously injured, or the casualties among troops from the rest of the British Empire.

▼ In 1915 volunteers were asked to sign up, on the understanding that single men would be called up to fight before any married men with children. There were still plenty of volunteers, as this queue at Southwark Town Hall shows.

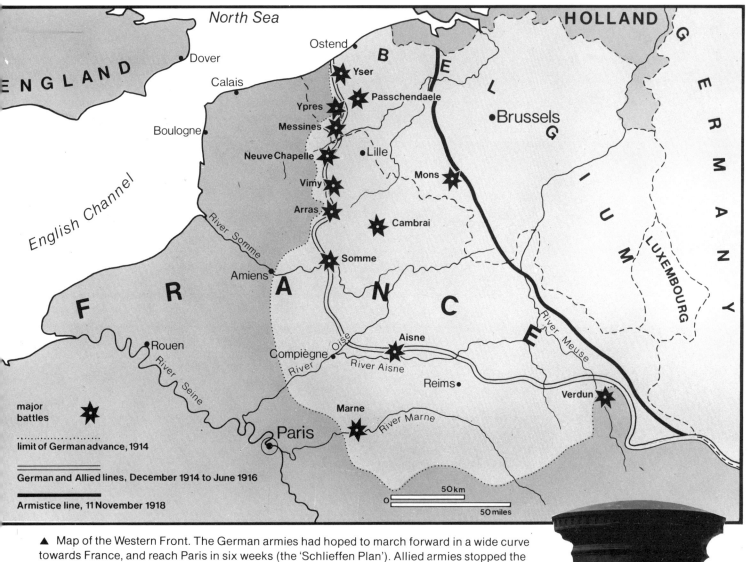

North Sea

HOLLAND

GERMANY

ENGLAND

Dover

Calais

Boulogne

English Channel

Ostend

BELGIUM

Yser

Passchendaele

Ypres

Messines

Neuve Chapelle

Lille

Brussels

Vimy

Mons

Arras

Cambrai

River Somme

Somme

Amiens

FRANCE

LUXEMBOURG

Rouen

River Seine

Compiègne

River Oise

Aisne

River Aisne

River Meuse

Reims

Verdun

major
battles

Marne

River Marne

Paris

limit of German advance, 1914

German and Allied lines, December 1914 to June 1916

Armistice line, 11 November 1918

50 km

0

50 miles

▲ Map of the Western Front. The German armies had hoped to march forward in a wide curve towards France, and reach Paris in six weeks (the 'Schlieffen Plan'). Allied armies stopped the Germans before they reached Paris. The map shows the main areas of battle on the Western Front during the four years of the war. Millions of men were killed or injured fighting over this small area of land.

▼ Bad weather made it hard to get supplies to men in the trenches. Here a horse-drawn water-cart is stuck in the mud.

▶ Posters were put up everywhere, even on the local pillar box, asking for recruits 'for the duration of the war'.

Are <u>YOU</u> in this?

DESIGNED BY LT. GEN. SIR R.S.S. BADEN POWELL

▲ Jack Cornwell, aged 16, served on the cruiser 'Chester' in the Battle of Jutland in May, 1916. Early in the fighting he was badly wounded but he stayed at his post even though men were being killed or injured all around him. He died of his wounds, and was awarded a posthumous Victoria Cross for his bravery.

◄ Baden-Powell, founder of the Boy Scout and Girl Guide movements, designed this famous poster.

▼ The number of casualties meant that many more hospital beds and nursing staff were needed. Schools and large houses were taken over by the government to serve as extra hospitals or convalescent homes.

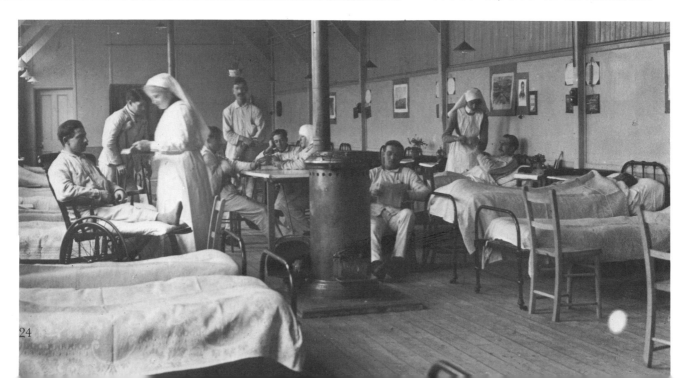

Conscription

Lord Kitchener was drowned in 1916, when his ship H.M.S. Hampshire was sunk. His call for volunteers had been answered by two and a half million men. But many men were killed and injured every day. Britain and her allies were attacking the Germans along the River Somme, in Northern France. On the first day of the attack, 60 000 British men had been killed or wounded.

The army could not rely on volunteers any longer. First single men, then married men with families were called up to join the army. There were 16 000 conscientious objectors who refused to fight on principle.

'Conchies', as the objectors were called, were despised as cowards and badly-treated. They had to go to a military court to explain why they did not want to fight. If their reasons were accepted, the objectors were given jobs on the land, in hospitals or in other non-fighting units. If the court did not accept their reasons, the objectors could be imprisoned, or put in uniform and sent to the Front.

Cowardice and desertion were crimes punishable by death. Men who disobeyed orders were tried by a Court Martial and executed by firing squad. Their families were never told how they had died. Later in the war, people began to realise that many of these soldiers had been suffering from 'shell shock' and had not really known what they were doing.

In Parliament, the Conservative and Liberal parties had formed a coalition government. Instead of only one party being in power, both parties worked together. They had raised extra taxes and taken control of farms, factories and other industries. Everyone had to help produce things needed for the war. But in 1916, the war was still dragging on.

Parliament decided that it needed a new leader. Mr Asquith was replaced by Lloyd George – the Prime Minister 'who could win the war'.

▼ Victoria Station became the scene of many farewells as troops waited to leave for France. Soldiers on leave also arrived at Victoria and convoys of wounded men were constantly passing through.

▲ In the early part of the war, the Royal Flying Corps was used mainly to report on enemy positions. The aeroplanes didn't have much sophisticated equipment and bombs were dropped from the cockpit by hand. Later, the Flying Corps was re-named the Royal Air Force, bombs were dropped by machinery and fighter planes were equipped with machine guns.

12. The right to serve, 1917

Women in wartime

Some men, such as miners, had jobs which were important for the war. They were not called up, although many had volunteered. But so many men were away fighting that there were not enough trained people to do the jobs needed at home. Those who were left behind started to do jobs which they had never been trained for. And nearly three million of these new workers were women.

Many women were employed to make guns and ammunition. It was hard and sometimes dangerous work. Handling chemicals affected the women's health, and there was always danger from explosions. But factory wages were higher than many girls had ever dreamed of earning before the war.

Thousands of women were needed to care for the wounded. Some were qualified nurses. Others were 'V.A.D.s', the voluntary helpers in the war hospitals.

Women were seen in unexpected uniforms. Sixteen thousand of them joined the Women's Land Army to work in farming or forestry. Women drove ambulances, became railway porters, swept the streets and delivered coal. For some jobs they even wore trousers. Jobs in business were also taken over by women, who found that they could do the work as well as men had done.

▼ A bus conductress: soon a familiar sight, these women were given their own uniform and nicknamed 'clippies'.

There would be no election until after the war. But now that women did so many important jobs, it was difficult for people to object to votes for women.

While women were working to provide guns and ammunition, British troops were still fighting on the Western Front. They had lost their Russian allies. Over 1 700 000 Russian soldiers had been killed during the war, and the Russian people were desperately short of food. Lenin and the other leaders of the Bolshevik Revolution had promised that they would take Russia out of the war. In November 1917, they signed a peace treaty with Germany.

Britain had also gained an ally. America was coming into the war. German submarines had attacked American ships and Woodrow Wilson, the President of the U.S.A., had decided that America could not stay neutral any longer.

▲ By June 1916, there were 150 000 women making munitions, thousands more would follow as soon as there were enough factories to employ them all. Women worked the same long hours as men, although some machines had to be adapted to suit their strength.

▼ The Women's Auxiliary Army Corps was formed in 1916, and attracted 50 000 'WAACs' in the first few months. Some served in France as cooks at army camps. It was a new experience for men in the army to be supervised by women.

Rationing

Civilian life in Britain was hard and gloomy. Many kinds of food were in short supply because British farmers could not produce enough. Before the war, these foods had been brought in from abroad. But this was no longer possible. German submarines had been attacking ships which carried supplies. Most of the food from abroad ended up at the bottom of the sea.

Food and many other goods, became more expensive. Money became worth much less and the gold sovereign was replaced by a paper pound note. There wasn't enough food for everyone, and those with more money were better able to pay the higher prices. By 1917, the government began to take control, trying to make sure that what little food there was would be fairly shared.

The price of basic foods, such as bread and potatoes, was kept down. Meals in hotels and restaurants were restricted. People could buy sugar only by registering at one particular shop. Most households had at least two days a week without meat. By January 1918, many butchers' shops and wholesale meat markets didn't bother to open. They had nothing to sell.

By February, rationing was introduced for almost all kinds of food. Every household was given a food card. This allowed people to buy small amounts of meat and groceries each week, for example, 4oz (113gms) of butter; 1½oz (42gms) of tea. When an item was bought, the shopkeeper would cross it off the food card.

Fish wasn't rationed, but it was difficult to find. There were often long queues at the shops. People were encouraged to grow their own vegetables for food, but women doing full-time jobs didn't have time to dig the allotments. Schoolchildren helped to grow more vegetables by digging up parks and sports grounds.

Newspapers suggested menus and shopping lists to make the best of rationing. In the spring of 1918, the papers seemed to have more bad news every day. The Germans had broken through the lines of British and Allied troops on the Western Front. Field Marshal Douglas Haig urged the troops to fight on to the end 'With our backs to the wall', because 'Victory will belong to the side which holds out the longest.'

By August the Allies had begun to move forward again. Without the men and supplies they needed, the German troops were forced back.

▲ 'Harvest of Battle', by Nevinson – one of the many famous paintings by war artists of the time. Artists, and poets such as Wilfred Owen and Siegfried Sassoon, tried to show people what the fighting was really like.

▶ A captured German U-boat. Since the early months of the war, these submarines had been torpedoing the merchant ships which carried food to Britain. The Germans hoped to force Britain to surrender by cutting off supplies of food and fuel.

▼ By 1918, everyone in Britain was given food cards. This meant that nobody could get more than the ration, however rich and powerful they were. The meat cards issued to the King and Queen were just like everyone else's.

▼ A poster asking people to save bread. According to government propaganda, if the 48 million people in Britain each saved one slice of bread a day, it would add up to 9 380 tonnes of bread a week, or two shiploads. It was estimated that twenty German submarines would be needed to sink that amount of bread!

THE KITCHEN IS THE TO VICTORY EAT LESS BREAD

The German commanders tried to make an agreement for peace, based on an American plan which President Wilson had drawn up. This would have allowed them to stop the war before they were forced to surrender. But the Allies would not accept the plan. They pressed on, taking prisoners and capturing guns and equipment.

German soldiers were deserting, and turning against their military commanders and the Kaiser. The Kaiser abdicated and fled to Holland. The Armistice was signed, and the war was officially over at 11 a.m. on 11 November 1918.

In London, guns fired blank charges to signal the end of the war. People rushed out of their homes, shops and offices to celebrate in the streets. Most town centres were crowded with people dancing and singing. But although the war was over at last, there were a lot of problems to be solved before people could live normally again.

14. Epidemic, 1919

'Back to normal'

Now that the war was over, people hoped that they could go back to living normal lives. 'Back to normal' was the slogan everywhere. But it was going to be impossible for people to live the way they had done before the war.

Soon after the Armistice, Lloyd George had called a general election. Women over the age of thirty had been allowed to vote; so had all men over twenty-one and even nineteen year olds who had been in the fighting. Conscientious objectors had not been allowed to vote.

Lloyd George was re-elected as the head of a new coalition government, with Conservatives and Liberals working together in Parliament. There were plans to hang the Kaiser, make Germany pay the full cost of the war and turn Britain into a 'land fit for heroes'. But none of this was to happen.

The government planned to slowly release men from the army when there were jobs for them. But the plan failed because soldiers wanted to go home to their families straight away. Over two million men came home to look for jobs. Many of them could not find work or a place to live.

There were food and fuel shortages. People who were cold and hungry had no resistance to disease. Many became seriously ill.

The previous year, thousands of soldiers and civilians had been killed by influenza. In February 1919, there was another outbreak of the disease. Three-quarters of the British population were affected and, altogether, 15 000 people were killed.

When the epidemic was at its worst, doctors and nurses fell ill, businesses and shops closed down, and public transport was in chaos.

People who caught influenza were told to go to bed and take aspirin. But often patients were so ill that the doctor had to be called in. Only the wage-earner in a family was covered by health insurance. If an elderly person, housewife or child fell ill, there would be a medical bill to pay.

The epidemic did not only affect Britain and those countries who had been involved in the war. In a few months, throughout the world thirty million deaths were caused by influenza. This was more than all those people who had been killed in the war.

The influenza epidemic showed people in Britain that better medical care and research into infectious diseases was badly needed. In the next twenty years, increased medical research would lead to a sharp drop in the number of people who died from tuberculosis, diphtheria and other serious diseases.

◀ The signing of the Treaty of Versailles, 1919. The terms of peace were decided mainly by Britain, France and the U.S.A. They made Germany accept the blame for having started the war. France wanted payment from Germany to make up for all the damage to French towns, farms and industries, but it would be impossible for one country to pay for all the damage.

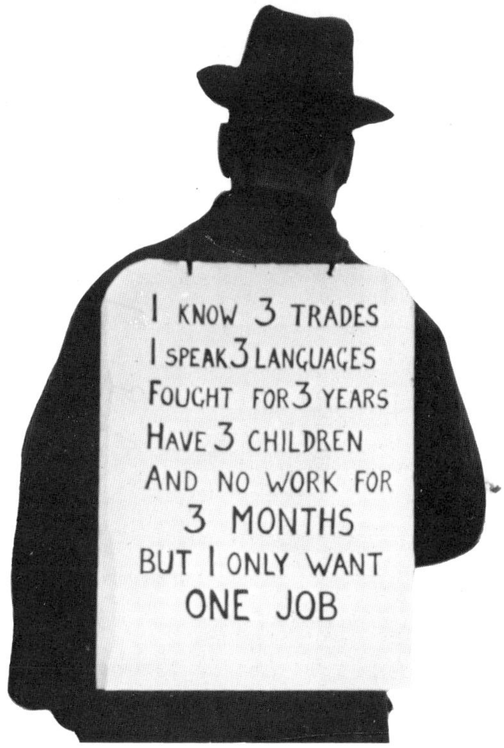

▼ Advertisement for a 'bronchitis kettle' designed to release warm vapours which would help influenza victims to breathe more easily. Patent medicines from the chemist were often cheaper than a visit from the doctor.

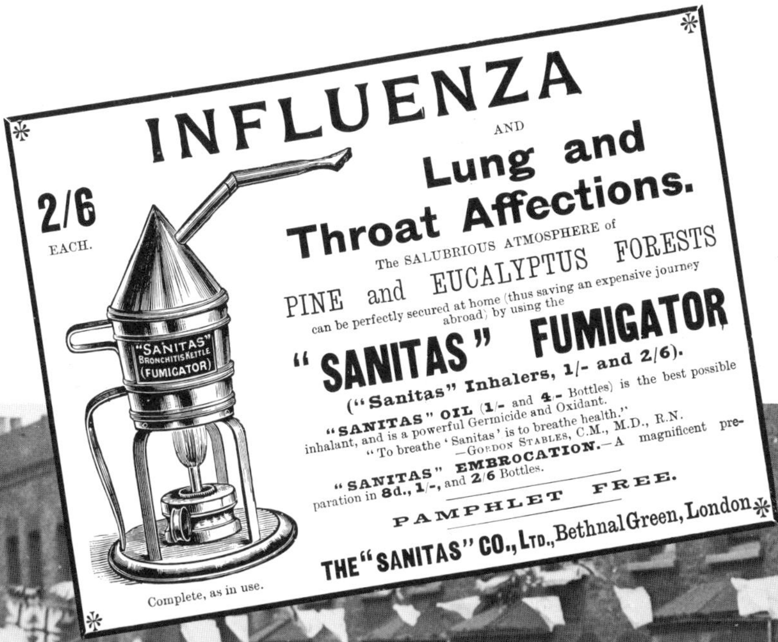

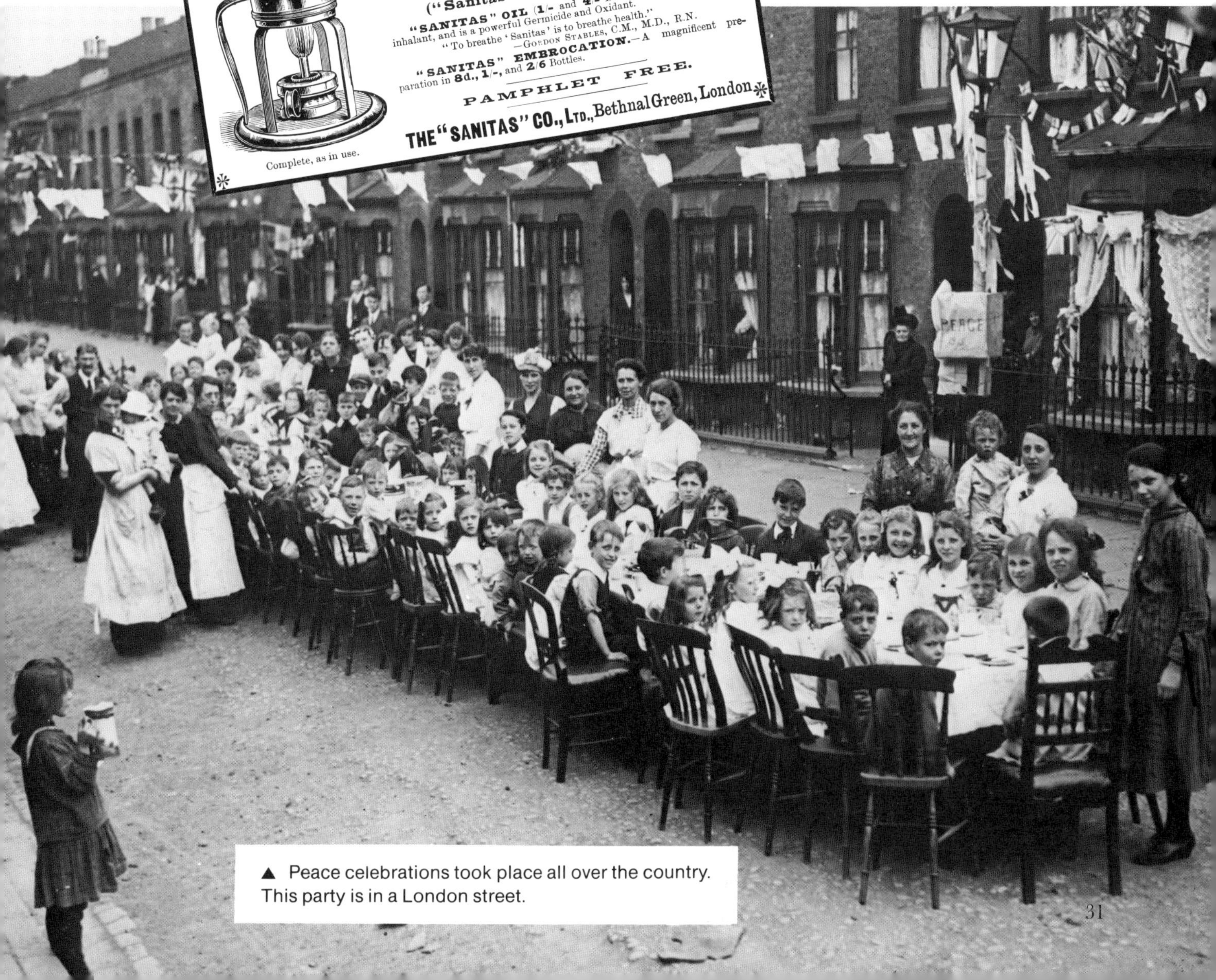

INFLUENZA
AND
Lung and Throat Affections.

2/6 EACH.

The SALUBRIOUS ATMOSPHERE of
PINE and EUCALYPTUS FORESTS
can be perfectly secured at home (thus saving an expensive journey abroad) by using the

"SANITAS" FUMIGATOR

("Sanitas" Inhalers, 1/- and 2/6).

"SANITAS" OIL (1/- and 4/- Bottles) is the best possible inhalant, and is a powerful Germicide and Oxidant.
"To breathe 'Sanitas' is to breathe health."
—GORDON STABLES, C.M., M.D., R.N.

"SANITAS" EMBROCATION.—A magnificent preparation in 8d., 1/-, and 2/6 Bottles.

PAMPHLET FREE.

THE "SANITAS" CO., LTD., Bethnal Green, London

Complete, as in use.

I KNOW 3 TRADES
I SPEAK 3 LANGUAGES
FOUGHT FOR 3 YEARS
HAVE 3 CHILDREN
AND NO WORK FOR
3 MONTHS
BUT I ONLY WANT
ONE JOB

▲ Ex-servicemen found it difficult to get jobs when they came home.

▲ Peace celebrations took place all over the country. This party is in a London street.

▲ Motor-cycles like this B.S.A. model allowed people to have cheap private transport. Ex-servicemen were awarded 'gratuities', small sums of money, when they left the army. Many of them used the money to buy their first motor-cycles.

▼ A home-made warning that a learner-driver was at the wheel, before there were any rules about L-plates and driving tests.

15. Hill-climb, 1920

Motoring

Before 1914 only the very rich had motor cars. During the war the army relied mainly on horse-drawn transport but motorised vehicles came to be used more and more.

In September 1916 Britain used the first armoured cars in battle. They were nicknamed 'tanks'. A Rolls-Royce 'Silver Ghost' car did National Service as an ambulance, and many officers took their civilian cars to the Front with them. The Motor Volunteer Corps supplied private cars with drivers for the war effort. Almost every type of commercial vehicle, from lorries to small vans, came in useful.

Hundreds of young soldiers were trained as mechanics and drivers. When they left the army, they bought small cars or motor-cycles. Motoring became a practical way of getting about, instead of just a hobby for the very rich.

During the war, British motor car production had almost stopped. Jowett, a company in Bradford, made munitions instead. But, like many other small firms, Jowett was making light cars again by 1920, at a rate of about twenty-five a week.

The first cheap mass-produced car was the Model T. It was made by an American company called Ford. In 1922, Ford sold a million Model Ts and in 1923 the yearly sales had gone up to three million.

Small family businesses could not compete with this kind of mass-production. British firms started to use Ford's methods to make their own cheap cars.

William Morris designed the two-seater Oxford and the four-seater Cowley. In 1922 Herbert Austin introduced the Baby Austin, or 'Austin Seven'. It could seat four people, took up no more garage space than a motor-bike and sidecar, and could reach 40 m.p.h. (64 km/h). But most important, it only cost £225.

Expensive luxury and sporting cars could reach much higher speeds. Bentley's 3-litre model cost £1 395 and could speed round a race-track at 80 m.p.h. (129 km/h).

On public roads, there was a speed limit of 20 m.p.h. (32 km/h), but no one took much notice of it. A driver's licence cost only five shillings (25p), and there was no need to take a test. There were no traffic lights in Britain, and no pedestrian crossings. Not surprisingly, there were a lot of road accidents!

Petrol was sold in cycle shops, chemists or even grocers. In 1920 the first filling-station was opened, at Aldermaston. Others soon followed. As roads improved, maps were printed. More and more people began to go on driving trips in their free time.

Motorised transport also affected people who did not have their own cars. The motor bus could provide public transport to rural areas, or be hired for outings. 'Charabanc' trips took people to parts of the country where there were no railway stations. Long-distance lorries began to carry goods which had been transported by railway.

Many ex-servicemen found work in the motor industry. These new jobs were badly needed. In the traditional 'heavy' industries, such as mining, jobs were now hard to find and did not pay very well.

▶ The 'Austin Seven'. In 1922 it cost £225.
▼ Motor-sports became popular. This photograph shows racing-driver, Arthur McDonald.

▲ Miners worked in dangerous conditions, and accidents were common. Here, families and friends wait outside the gates of a Birmingham colliery (1908) after a mine shaft has collapsed, trapping the men inside.

16. Roof-fall, 1921

Mining

Before the war coal mining was one of Britain's most important industries. Whole towns and villages earned a living by working in the local coal pits. Often, a man and his sons would work in the same mine.

It was hard, tiring work. The miners' tools hadn't changed much since the eighteenth century. At the beginning of the First World War, most miners still hewed coal with a pick, and levered slabs away with a crowbar. Only a very small amount of coal was cut using machinery. The owners of the mines were not able or willing to buy the expensive machines which were needed.

Some miners had to work crouching or lying down in the dark cramped tunnels. They were always in danger from roof-falls, explosions or flooding. The coal-dust they breathed in every day affected their lungs.

During the war the government took control of many industries, including the coal mines. This was so that everyone could help produce things which were needed for the war. When the war ended, the owners of the mines wanted to manage their own businesses again, without interference from the government.

The miners wanted the government to carry on running the coal mines. They wanted the mines to be nationalised. Only the government had enough money to buy new machinery and make the improvements which were so badly needed.

A special committee, called the Sankey Commission, was set up to advise the government what to do. In 1919, they advised the government to keep control of the mines.

To prevent strikes, the government had been adding extra money to the miners' wages so that they would have enough to live on. But in 1921, sales of British coal suddenly dropped. Other countries were selling coal more cheaply. Germany was paying war-debts in coal. British coal cost more than people were willing to pay for it.

The government decided that they could not afford to lose any more money. They handed control of the mines back to the owners.

To save money, the owners cut the miners' wages. This meant that miners and their families were worse off than they had been before the war. Even then, they had been very badly paid.

The miners asked other Trade Unions to help them. The Trade Unions of miners, railway men and transport workers had already agreed that they would help each other in disputes about wages and conditions. They decided that they would all go on strike together to protest against the miners' wage cuts. But on 'Black Friday', 15 April 1921, the agreement broke down. The miners had to go on strike alone.

After two months, Parliament voted to set aside ten million pounds to help the mining industry keep going. But the miners had to go back to work on lower wages.

People working in jobs such as ship building, engineering and textile manufacture also had their pay cut. Jobs were hard to find. Many families had to try to live on the fifteen shillings (75p) a week which they got as unemployment benefit.

The worst unemployment and wage cuts were in the north, and in other areas where people had jobs in the old 'heavy' industries, such as mining, engineering and shipbuilding. Families began moving to the south or midlands to look for jobs in new industries.

▲ Strikes for better wages and conditions led to coal shortages. Even miners' families could not get enough coal. During a strike in the winter of 1912, these women and children picked coal out of the waste thrown from coal trucks.

▼ Miners' children queuing for free bread during the miners' strike of 1921.

17. The electric light, 1922

Electricity and new industries

In the midlands and the south of England some new industries were being started. Most of these were based on scientific ideas which had been developed during wartime.

Factories had been built to make chemicals which Britain could not buy from Germany during the war. In peacetime, these factories developed new ways of using chemicals. They made rayon, disinfectant, plastics, synthetic rubber and a wide range of other products, including the gases which were used inside electric lamps.

Factories were beginning to use electricity, but most streets and houses were lit by gas. 'Town gas' was owned by local councils. Electricity for houses was supplied by some councils and by small private companies.

This meant that two houses in the same area might get their electricity from different places and even use different voltages. Costs varied too, but some councils started 'assisted wiring schemes' which allowed people to pay in instalments.

In 1920, a 'futuristic' all-electric house had been on show at the Ideal Home Exhibition. It contained many new labour-saving devices such as vacuum cleaners, electric irons, and electric fires and cookers so that women wouldn't have to carry coal or have the chimney swept.

Middle-class women flocked to buy the new labour-saving gadgets, because domestic servants were getting hard to find. Girls who might have been housemaids before the war were now finding jobs in factories.

Demand went up for cables, telephone apparatus, lamps and ignition sets for motor cars. This created many new jobs, but there were still at least a million people unemployed.

The unemployment insurance scheme which provided the Dole could not cope with the problem. It had been intended to help men and women for a few weeks when they were between jobs, not to keep them for months or even years.

People could only claim the Dole for a certain time. After that, they had to claim money from their local councils. The areas worst hit by unemployment had the least money to give and councils got into debt.

▲ An advertisement for electric lights.

ELECTRICAL DEPARTMENT
Labour-Saving Devices Which Save Both Time and Money

Please state Voltage when Ordering

REPAIRS

If its anything Electrical write or 'phone Harrods

Prompt and highly skilled attention

E 69 MAGNET ELECTRIC OSCILLATING FAN
Bracket or Desk type
An exceptionally powerful type of Fan which can be adjusted according to requirements
£5 18 6

NEW MODEL THE 'THOR' ELECTRIC WASHING MACHINE
An electric Washer and Wringer combined. Clothes can be thoroughly washed in the New 'Thor' Model in from 3 to 5 minutes, and the running costs are so low as to be almost negligible £29 17 6
Complete with Ironing Attachment £39 17 6
Complete booklet of Washing Machines forwarded on application

EL 5702 'MAGNET' COOKER
for a family of 4-6 persons. Cast iron door, door frames, hot table, etc., and with sheet steel body. There are 2 enclosed boiling plates, and a griller or toaster, spacious oven total loading 5,500 Watts. The oven and boiling plates are controlled by switches giving full, half and quarter heat. Price £18 0 0
Write for booklet showing full range of models

E 66 MAGNET ELECTRIC FAN
Desk or Bracket type, with current consumption of 34 watts
£4 6 6
State Voltage when Ordering

EL 555 'PROTOS' ELECTRIC FLOOR POLISHER
For cleaning and polishing Linoleum, Parquet Floors, and Painted Floors. 2 brushes covering 12 ins. of floor. Price complete with 25 ft. cord, plug adapter, and 1 set of polishing brushes
£13 13 0
Other makes in stock

HOOVER
The Greater Hoover. Model 700 ... ... £17 17 0
A more popular priced Hoover Model (543) ... £13 13 0
Dusting tools for both models £3 3 0
Either may be had for £1 down
Only the Hoover embodies the exclusive deep-cleaning principle of Positive Agitation. Hangings, carpet, upholstery, are cleaned easier, quicker and more thoroughly
Supplied with new Floor Polishing Attachment £2 0 0 extra

EL 28 MAGNET ELECTRIC WASHING MACHINE
Washing day without labour. Saves time and money Washes 6 sheets or their equivalent in 15 minutes £42 0 0
Attachments are available for the machine so that it can be used for making ice-cream, mincing and sausage making, knife cleaning, making butter, etc.

EL 71 MAGNET ELECTRIC MASSAGE VIBRATOR
This is a valuable appliance, whether for medical use or simply as a toilet vibrator. The equipment includes six different types of applicators. Price £4 15 0

ALL PRICES ARE SUBJECT TO MARKET FLUCTUATIONS

HARRODS LTD
Telephone SLOANE 1234
Telegrams 'EVERYTHING HARRODS LONDON'
LONDON S W 1

◀ This page from a Harrods catalogue shows some of the electrical appliances which were being developed during the 1920s. The new industry provided work in factories, and jobs for demonstrators who could show the customers how to use their new gadgets.

Ideal for Dance Wear

THIS model was expressly introduced to meet the demand for a corset, comfortable in wear, without busks or boning, for Jazz dancing, and has sold very largely since for other purposes.

It laces at the back, and the front section is made of open wove elastic, allowing absolute freedom to the muscles of the abdomen, and giving all the necessary support required. It is an exceptionally suitable model for extreme exercise. It has two pairs of suspenders and is made in both White and Rose.

The depth under arms is 11 in. and the depth of the front piece is 9 in.
In sizes 20-28. Model No. 427.

23/6

Write to Dept. "G" for art folder "Examples of Modern Corsets"—a beautifully illustrated brochure—send post free, together with name of nearest agent.

"Art steps in where nature fails."

Worth's Corsets, Ltd.,
3, Hamsell Street, London, E.C.1

▲ Light-weight artificial fabrics were beginning to take the place of natural-fibre materials such as wool or silk. In 1924, artificial silk was given its own name 'Rayon'. Another version, 'Celanese', could be used for blouses and underclothes.

Lloyd George became less and less popular. Most of the improvements he had promised could not be carried out properly because the government had so little money. The government had cut spending on education, defence and housing. Even ex-servicemen had lost their pensions. Lloyd George's plan to separate Ulster in the north of Ireland from the Irish Free State in the south was opposed by many people and lead to fighting between British troops and Republicans in Ireland.

The Conservative Party decided that they would not work with the Liberal Party any more. There was a general election. The Conservatives won the election with the slogan 'tranquillity'. Bonar Law became the first Conservative Prime Minister since 1906. He was replaced by Stanley Baldwin in May 1923.

▼ The Irish rebellion: an arms search in Dublin. Civil war broke out in 1922, after the British government had founded the Irish Free State in the South. Although the new state had an independent government in Dublin, it was a Dominion of Britain under the British King or Queen, like New Zealand and Australia. Some Irish Republicans accepted this settlement, but others wanted complete independence from Britain.

The family wireless

For over twenty years, the wireless had been used to send messages from one place to another. At first, messages could only be sent by Morse code. In 1910, a wireless message from ship to shore brought about the arrest of the notorious murderer Dr Crippen. When the Titanic sank, in 1912, wireless messages helped to save lives. Later, it became possible to transmit speech or music. But people didn't listen to programmes on the wireless the way we listen to radio programmes today.

In 1922, the British Broadcasting Company was formed to broadcast the first regular wireless programmes in Britain. The money needed to run the B.B.C. would come from wireless licence fees and a tax on sales of wireless sets.

Everyone wanted to listen to the new broadcasts. Wireless equipment could be an expensive valve-and-battery receiver in a smart cabinet, or a simple crystal set homemade by an enthusiastic schoolboy.

The crystal set did not need batteries. An outside aerial conducted the signal. The set was tuned by touching the crystal with the 'cat's whisker', a springy wire. If anyone in the family slammed a door (or even sneezed!) reception could be lost. The signal was so weak that it could only be heard through headphones. But all over the country, people could tune in to the same programmes.

Who would decide which programmes to broadcast? Radio manufacturers could not be in charge of programme content. Nor could advertisers, or the government. The B.B.C was given the job of deciding which programmes they would broadcast. They were to include as many aspects of entertainment and education as possible. John Reith was appointed as the first General Manager of the B.B.C.

There were some things which the B.B.C. was not allowed to do. News could not be broadcast before seven o'clock in the evening, as newspaper owners were afraid they would lose sales. Sporting events could be covered as long as listeners weren't told the results! On Sundays, comedy, light music and popular talks were not allowed.

▼ A crystal set had to be tuned by 'tickling the cat's whisker'. It was a cheap way of 'listening in', as a set cost only 7/6d (35p).

None of this could spoil the thrill of having a wireless. Just before six o'clock, children would settle arguments over who should wear which set of headphones. Then they would tune into 'Children's Hour', presented by the B.B.C.'s team of 'Uncles' and 'Aunties'.

Throughout 1924, a new relay station was opened each month. By the summer of 1925, the Daventry station was opened. It was the biggest in the world. Now, wireless could be heard, even on crystal sets, by most people in Britain.

In 1924, there was another general election and the first 'party political broadcasts' were made on wireless. The party leaders, Stanley Baldwin (Conservative), Asquith (Liberal), and Ramsey MacDonald (Labour) all made speeches. Baldwin used a quiet conversational voice for the microphone. The other two spoke as if they were talking to crowds of people at a meeting, not to individual listeners at home. The Conservatives won and politicians learned, if they didn't know already, just how powerful the wireless could be.

◄ In 1923, the Grand National train was fitted with a wireless saloon. A loudspeaker was supplied, so listeners did not need headphones.

▶ The cover of the first issue of 'The Radio Times', 28 September 1923. Within two years, the B.B.C. was transmitting programmes to most regions of the British Isles. In 1927, the British Broadcasting Company was renamed the British Broadcasting Corporation, paid for only from licence fees.

▼ Children were among the keenest followers of wireless broadcasting. Before the B.B.C. was founded, the Marconi Wireless Telephony was being demonstrated to young people (May 1919).

▲ Rudolph Valentino with Vilma Banky in 'The Son of the Sheik'.

▼ Dancing the charleston.

19. The roaring 'twenties, 1925

The charleston era

Two of the most popular songs in the 'twenties were 'I want to be happy' and 'Ain't we got fun?' Life had been hard and gloomy for a long time and everyone had sad memories of the war. Young people who had enough money to spend, tried to forget the last few years and not think too much about the future. They went to parties, played practical jokes and enjoyed shocking their elders.

The old-fashioned waltz was replaced by reckless new dances like the shimmy-shake, the black-bottom and the charleston. Older people thought the new dances were immoral, especially as the girls seemed to be only half-dressed. The dance halls were filled with girls in 'flapper dresses' with short skirts above the knee, although their mothers would have been embarrassed to show an ankle.

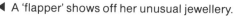

◀ A 'flapper' shows off her unusual jewellery.　　▲ A tennis party in 1922.

▲ One of the more outrageous fashions for young men in 1925, 'Oxford bags' were trousers made with yards of extra material.

Feminine curves were out of fashion. A flat-chested girl was considered stylish, and modern clothes were designed for her boyish figure. Girls had their hair cut short, first 'bobbed' then 'shingled'. A few even wore the outrageous 'Eton Crop', which made them look like schoolboys.

They wore lots of make-up, too, which older people thought indecent. Some girls even smoked cigarettes. They drank cocktails, powerful mixed drinks with odd names like 'Nose Dive' and 'Corpse Reviver'.

There was a new craze for jazz music. Ex-servicemen bought clarinets and saxophones, and formed their own jazz bands. Gramophone records were imported from America, bringing sounds of Dixieland and Broadway musicals.

Films were brought over from America, too. For a few pence, people could go to the cinema and see the stars of the silent films from Hollywood – Rudolph Valentino and Gloria Swanson in romantic films, or Charlie Chaplin and Buster Keaton in slapstick comedies.

Those with more money went to the theatre to see the latest revues and plays. Noel Coward was one of the most popular writers. Most of his plays were comedies, but they also showed some of the worries and confusion which people felt in the 'twenties. This is part of one of his songs, from 'On With the Dance':

> 'In lives of leisure
> The craze for pleasure
> Steadily grows.
> Cocktails and laughter,
> But what comes after?
> Nobody knows . . .'

On strike

Not everyone had enough money to forget their troubles by going to parties and the theatre. Many people were out of work, or were paid very low wages for long hours.

In spite of their strike in 1921, the miners were still badly paid. But in 1926 the mine-owners decided to cut wages even more. They wanted to make British coal cheaper so that they could sell it to European countries. The miners were told that they would have to work longer hours for less money.

The miners refused and invented the slogan 'Not a penny off the pay, not a minute on the day'. To avoid a strike, the government provided ten million pounds to keep the miners' wages at the same level for the time being.

A Royal Commission was appointed to try to solve the problem. They offered improvements in the future, but said that the miners' wages should be cut. Government money for wages would stop on 30 April 1926. The miners called a strike for 1 May.

This time the other Trade Unions decided that they would help the miners. They prepared for a General Strike. On 4 May, for the first time in Britain's history, the country was brought to a standstill by strikes. There were no trains, no buses or trams, no noise from factories, no activity in gas works or power stations, no movement in the docks, and no newspapers in which to read about what was happening.

The government called in troops, special constables and volunteers to keep essential services going. Students drove buses and trains, manned railway signal boxes and loaded lorries. The navy was sent to work in power stations. The army escorted lorry-loads of food from the docks to a huge central depot in Hyde Park.

Those who supported the strike were angry that their jobs were being done by troops and volunteers. Special constables were unpopular, too. These were mainly business or professional men. They were given an armband and a baton, and their job was to help volunteers to get through the strikers' picket lines and demonstrations.

As the days went by, support for the miners began to fade away. Motorists were offering lifts and lorries were moving food. The trains gradually began running again and timetables were announced by wireless. The B.B.C. broadcast news bulletins as there were no newspapers apart from the 'British Gazette', produced by the government, and 'The British Worker', the Trade Union news sheet.

After nine days, the General Strike was called off. The miners stayed on strike alone until the following autumn. They went back to work on even lower wages.

Younger leaders of the Trade Union movement had learned a lot from the General Strike. They knew that they needed a government which would support them. In 1929, for the first time, the Labour Party would win the general election.

◀ A 'black-leg' bus is driven through London by a volunteer. Barbed wire has been tied across the bonnet to stop demonstrators from crowding round. A special constable and a uniformed police officer ride with the driver to ward off attacks.

▲ Troops ride through the streets of London escorting a food convoy from the strike-bound docks to the Hyde Park depot.

▼ The Royal Air Force delivered mail during the strike.

Who was who

Here are some of the interesting people who were alive during 1902-1926. If you want to find out more about them, use an encyclopedia or see if your library has a biography.

Asquith, Herbert Henry (1852-1928)
Barrister and Liberal M.P., Home Secretary, Chancellor of the Exchequer, then Prime Minister 1908-1916. He formed a coalition government in wartime, but was forced to resign in 1916. Created Earl of Oxford 1925.

Austin, Sir Herbert (1866-1941)
Engineer making sheep-shearing machinery who founded his motor car business in 1890. Made guns and aircraft during the war and was knighted in 1917. Became a major car manufacturer with the 'Baby Austin'. Served as M.P. for King's Norton, 1919-1924.

Baden-Powell, Lt. Gen. Sir R.S.S. (1857-1941)
Served with the British Army, mainly in India and South Africa, distinguished in the Boer War by his defence of Mafeking (October-Jan 1900). Retired in 1910 to further the Boy Scout and Girl Guide movements which he had founded. Made a peer in 1929.

Cavell, Edith (1865-1915)
English nurse appointed Matron in Brussels, 1907, where she stayed despite the German invasion. Accused of harbouring French, British and Belgian soldiers and assisting their escape, she was condemned to death by the German military authorities and executed by firing squad, an outrage which angered British people.

Churchill, Winston L.S. (1874-1965)
Served in the army, then covered the South African war as a journalist. Entered Parliament in 1900 as a Conservative but became a Liberal for the 1906 election. He held many cabinet posts before, during and after the war, when he rejoined the Conservatives (1924). He was not made Prime Minister until the Second World War crisis of 1940.

Collins, Michael (1890-1922)
Irish politician who was imprisoned for his part in the Easter Rising, 1916. Elected M.P. in 1918 for the Sinn Fein Party which broke away from Westminster and met in Dublin. Head of the Irish Republican Army 1920-21, he helped to negotiate a settlement with Britain for an Irish Free State, but was killed in an ambush by Republicans.

De Valera, Eamon (1883-1975)
Irish Republican born in New York, his American citizenship saved him from execution after the Easter Rising in Dublin, 1916. He was Sinn Fein's leader, and after escaping from Lincoln Gaol he raised funds by a propaganda tour of the U.S.A. Sinn Fein wanted complete freedom from Britain, for all Ireland, including Ulster. De Valera, as President of the Irish Free State, 1932-1948, broke all ties with Britain.

Elgar, Sir Edward (1857-1934)
British musician and composer. Two of his most famous works were 'Enigma Variations' and 'The Dream of Gerontius'. He also wrote 'Coronation Ode' (1902) from which came 'Land of Hope and Glory', soon to be heard throughout the Empire. Much of his music was inspired by the quiet Edwardian countryside.

Haig, Earl Douglas (1861-1928)
A career-soldier, with the rank of Lt.Colonel by the turn of the century. Served in South Africa until peace was made with the Boers, then in India and at the War Office. Went with the British Expeditionary Force as a General in 1914. Promoted to Field-Marshal in 1917 and given an earldom in 1919, he spent his later years helping ex-servicemen.

Harmsworth, Sir Alfred (1865-1922)
Journalist and newspaper owner. Published the 'Daily Mail' (1896) and 'Daily Mirror' (1903), the first 'popular' newspapers, that cost a halfpenny. He became Lord Northcliffe in 1905, acquired 'The Times' in 1908 and owned 'The Observer' 1905-11.

Kipling, Rudyard (1865-1936)
British writer and traveller, published poems and stories, including books for children 'Stalky and Co.', 'Kim', 'Just-So Stories', 'The Jungle Book' and, after the war, 'Land and Sea Tales for Scouts and Guides', among many other works. He was awarded the Nobel Prize for literature in 1907.

Kitchener, Herbert Horatio (1850-1916)
British soldier, explorer, map-maker, Governor-General in the Sudan, aide-de-camp to Queen Victoria, and Commander-in-Chief from 1900 in the Boer War. He was made Lord Kitchener after ten years in India and time spent travelling the Empire. In 1914, he became Secretary of State for War. He was drowned when H.M.S. Hampshire was sunk in 1916.

Lawrence, Thomas Edward (1888-1935)
Scholar, soldier and explorer who became known as 'Lawrence of Arabia'. From 1915 he was organising Arab tribesmen in battle against the Turks. He often disagreed with British authorities. In 1919 he left the Paris Peace Conference in disgust, and in 1922 enlisted as an Air Force mechanic under the name T.E. Shaw. He was killed when his motorcycle crashed.

▼ T.E. Lawrence.

Susanne Lenglen, tennis star and [w]omen's singles champion at [W]imbledon from 1919-1923, and in [19]25. Less restrictive clothing helped [w]omen to succeed in sports.

[L]enin, Vladimir Ilyich Ulyanov (1870-1924)
[R]ussian law student who took the name of [L]enin. He was exiled to Siberia in 1895 after [fo]unding a 'Union for the liberation of the [w]orking-class' at St. Petersburg. Released in [19]00, he lived for a few years in Paris and [Lo]ndon, where he met Trotsky. He also lived [in] Switzerland. The German Government [sm]uggled him back into Russia to lead the [Bo]lshevik Revolution in October 1917. He [m]ade peace with Germany in 1918.

[Ll]oyd, Marie (1870-1922)
[En]glish music-hall artist. She was born in the [Ea]st End of London and worked in Drury [La]ne pantomime, with songs like 'My Old [M]an', and 'One of the Ruins that Cromwell [Kn]ocked About a Bit'. Her comedy was [co]nsidered too vulgar for the first Royal [Va]riety Performance, but she was a popular [st]ar for thirty years.

[Ll]oyd George, David (1863-1945)
[So]n of a poor Welsh schoolmaster who died [yo]ung, David Lloyd George was brought up [by] an uncle. His family were members of the [lo]cal Chapel. Lloyd George entered Parlia[m]ent in 1890. As Chancellor of the Exchequer [in] Asquith's Liberal government from 1908, [he] came into conflict with the House of Lords [wh]en they rejected his 'People's Budget'. In [sp]ite of opposition, he introduced old age [pe]nsions and a National Health Insurance [Ac]t (1911) to help the unemployed. During [th]e war he was put in charge of Munitions, [the]n made Prime Minister of the coalition [go]vernment in 1916. After the Armistice, he [hel]ped to shape the Treaty of Versailles, on [wh]ich peace in Europe was to be based. He [pr]omised 'a land fit for heroes', but Britain's [tra]de was depressed, and war debts had to be [p]aid. He tried to settle the Irish question by [se]parating Ulster in the north from the Irish [Fr]ee State in the south. In 1922, Conserva[tiv]es withdrew support from his coalition and [he] was forced to resign. The Liberal Party [wa]s divided, and although Lloyd George [sta]yed active in politics, his influence was [ne]ver as great again.

[Ow]en, Wilfred Edward Salter (1893-1918)
[Fro]m a middle-class family who fell on hard [tim]es, Owen left school in 1911. He worked [as] assistant to an Oxfordshire vicar, a [lan]guage tutor in France, and enlisted in the [arm]y in 1915. His poetry reflects the horror of [wa]r; his parents heard of his death in action [as] Armistice bells rang.

Pankhurst, Emmeline (1858-1928)
Suffragette who, with her daughters Christabel and Sylvia, helped to found the Women's Social and Political Union. Was arrested, imprisoned and released on health grounds many times between 1908 and 1913. During the war she turned to organising recruitment and munitions.

Redmond, John (1851-1918)
Irish politician, a leader of the Irish party in Parliament in 1891. After the General Election of 1910, Liberals depended on Irish support. Redmond supported Asquith's plan for Home Rule for Ireland (1912-14). His death left the way open for Sinn Fein Republicans.

Scott, Robert Falcon (1868-1912)
British explorer who commanded the National Antarctic Expedition, 1901-1904. In 1910 he sailed for the Antarctic on the 'Terra Nova' hoping to be first at the South Pole. Beaten to the Pole by the Norwegian, Amundsen, Scott and his companions were trapped by a blizzard on the return journey and died before they could be rescued.

Shaw, George Bernard (1856-1950)
Irish dramatist, early believer in Socialism, member of the Fabian Society, who began his career as a journalist and critic in London. His plays put forward Socialist ideas, as well as being popular entertainment. 'Pygmalion' is perhaps his best-known play. He was awarded the Nobel Prize for literature in 1925.

Sopwith, Sir Thomas O.M. (1888-   )
Trained as an engineer, in 1910 he won the Baron de Forest prize of £4000 for a flight from Kent to Belgium (304km in 3½ hours). During the Great war his company, Sopwith Aviation, designed and built aircraft, like the Sopwith Camel, and seaplanes for the British government. Knighted 1953.

Wells, Herbert George (1866-1946)
British novelist. A draper's assistant who won scholarships to study science, graduated with honours then became a teacher and journalist. His books portray life and problems of the time, and in some cases (eg. 'The War In The Air') predicted future events. Author of 'The Invisible Man', 'The First Men in the Moon', 'Kipps' and 'The History of Mr. Polly', among others.

45

Some important events 1902-1926

1902

End of the Boer War.
Coronation of Edward VII.
Arthur Balfour Prime Minister
(Conservative).
Local school boards replaced by local
government (councils) as education
authorities.

1903

Joseph Chamberlain and the Tariff Reform
League recommended taxing imports.
Erskine Childers wrote 'The Riddle Of The
Sands', a spy thriller suggesting Germany
might invade Britain.
In America, Orville and Wilbur Wright flew a
petrol-engined aeroplane for a distance of
36 metres. The flight lasted 12 seconds at a
height of 3.5 metres.
Motor taxi-cabs appeared in London.
Motoring speed limit raised to 20 m.p.h.

1904

Theodore Roosevelt elected President of
U.S.A.
The Committee of Imperial Defence set out
to improve British Army organisation after
the Boer War had revealed weaknesses.
The Daily Mirror was founded by Alfred
Harmsworth.
Invention of the photo-electric cell, the
ultra-violet lamp, and the thermionic radio
valve.
J. M. Barrie's 'Peter Pan' was produced.

1905

Balfour resigned. Liberals, with Campbell-
Bannerman as Prime Minister, came to
power.
A new party was formed to secure Home
Rule for Ireland: 'Sinn Fein', meaning
'Ourselves Alone'.
Motor-buses were tried in London.

1906

General Election ended in a landslide
victory for Liberals.
H.M.S. *Dreadnought* launched, the first
modern battleship, speed 21 km/h.
Workmen's Compensation Act made
employers pay compensation to workers for
accidents at work.
Rolls-Royce Ltd. founded.
Education authorities were to provide
school meals for children in need.

1907

Edward VII visited Tsar Nicholas II. Alliance
formed, between France, Russia, and
Britain.
Territorial Army introduced by Haldane, the
British War Minister.
Boy Scout movement founded.
Medical inspections of schoolchildren
began.
In Britain, women were allowed to serve on
local councils. Norway gave women the
right to vote, the first European country to
do so.
New Zealand became a British Dominion
(from having been a Victorian colony).

1908

Asquith succeeded as Prime Minister
(Liberal) after Campbell-Bannerman. He
held the post until 1916.
The Children's Act aimed to protect
children from neglect and set up separate
courts and treatment for juvenile offenders.
Kenneth Grahame published 'The Wind In
The Willows'.
250,000 suffragettes attended a Hyde Park
rally.
The Olympic Games were held in London.

1909

Lloyd George, as Chancellor of the
Exchequer, had his Budget passed by the
Commons but rejected by the House of
Lords.
French airman, Bleriot, flew from Calais to
Dover in 37 minutes. Farman made the first
100-mile flight. Sir A.V. Roe began aircraft
manufacture in Britain.
W.H. Taft became U.S. President (until
1913).

1910

Death of Edward VII. George V became
King.
British general election returned Liberals
with a reduced majority. Maximum time
between general elections was reduced
from 7 to 5 years. But another election
(December) was needed to settle issues of
the House of Lords and Home Rule.
First Labour Exchanges opened in Britain.

1911

Strikes and industrial unrest in Britain.
Coal Mines Act: no boy under 14 would be
allowed to work below ground.
The National Insurance Act provided
10 shillings (50p) a week for six months
during a worker's illness.
Members of Parliament were to receive
salaries of £400 a year.
Temperature in London reached 100° F on
9th August.

1912

Ulster Unionists rejected plans for Home
Rule for Ireland.
Titanic sank after it collided with an iceberg
1,513 lives were lost.
Shops Act gave shop assistants a half-day
holiday a week.
Suffragettes stepped up action by
damaging property and attacking M.P.s.
War in the Balkan countries.
The Royal Flying Corps was founded.
The Post Office took over British telephone
systems.

1913

The 'Cat and Mouse' Act provided for
temporary release of prisoners on hunger
strike. They could be re-arrested later.
Irish Home Rule Bill, passed by House of
Commons, but rejected by House of Lords.
Proclamation banned the sending of arms
to Ireland.
Sir Edward Carson led Ulster Unionist
resistance to Home Rule: John Redmond's
Irish Nationalist party supported the Liberal
party in order to get Home Rule.
Woodrow Wilson became U.S. President
(until 1921).
Russia entered the war in the Balkans.

1914

Opening of the Panama Canal.
June 28th: Austrian Archduke, Francis
Ferdinand, assassinated in Sarajevo.
August 1st: Germany declared war on
Russia.
August 3rd: Germany declared war on
France and invaded Belgium.
August 4th: Britain declared war on
Germany.
British Expeditionary Force sent to France.
The Retreat from Mons was followed by the
Battles of the Marne, the Aisne, and the first
Battle of Ypres.
German ships bombarded English coastal
towns.
The first bomb was dropped on Britain.

1915

Continual fighting along the Western Front
Germany blockaded Britain by intensive
submarine warfare. British blockade of
Germany.
Battle of Neuve Chapelle.
Germans first used poison gas.
First Zeppelin attack on London.
Nurse Edith Cavell's execution.
German U-boat torpedoed the Lusitania,
(1198 dead, including many Americans).

916

ilitary conscription introduced.
nn Fein Easter rebellion in Dublin leads to
kecution of ringleaders.
ne Battle of Verdun (February-December).
ne Battle of Jutland.
.M.S. *Hampshire* sunk, with Kitchener
board.
ummer Time' (Daylight saving)
troduced.
ank of England issued £1 and 10 shilling
otes.
rst use of the 'tank', by Heavy Machine
un Corps (later Royal Tank Corps).
squith resigned, Lloyd George became
rime Minister of a coalition government.

917

attles of Messines, Passchendaele,
ambrai.
od shortages in Britain. Bread and sugar
tioning were introduced.
evolutions in Russia (March and October);
e Bolsheviks seized control.
ermans used mustard gas.
e British Royal Family assumed the name
Windsor because people were so hostile
German names.
e U.S.A. entered the war against
ermany.
n the Southern Front, Allenby captured
rusalem from the Turks.

918

od rationing and price controls were
roduced.
ssia surrendered to Germany. Allies
gan to push back German troops on the
estern Front. German Navy mutinied.
mistice was signed.
orld-wide influenza epidemic began.
itish general election resulted in a
ajority for a coalition government, led by
oyd George.
men over 21 and all women over 30 had
e vote.

919

e Versailles Peace Conference. Heavy
nalties were imposed on Germany.
dy Astor became the first woman M.P.
e Central Electricity Commission was set
to supply cheap electricity.
e Sankey Commission was set up to
estigate the coal industry.
ock and Brown flew the Atlantic and a
ly London-Paris air service began.

1920

Two Irish Parliaments were offered, in
Belfast and Dublin. There were violent
protests by Republicans, the 'Black and
Tans' were sent to Ireland to repress
protests.
Ghandi launched a campaign of civil
disobedience to British rule in India.
First public broadcasting station in Britain
was opened by Marconi.
Oxford University admitted women to
degrees.

1921

Over two million out of work in Britain.
Coal prices fell. Mines no longer under
government control.
Miners' strike.
Out-of-work donations to ex-soldiers
ended. (March).
British truce with Sinn Fein.

1922

Geddes Economy Committee advised
severe cuts in public spending, on defence,
housing, and education.
Insulin first used to treat diabetes.
The British Broadcasting Company was
formed.
Mussolini's Fascists took control in Italy.
Stalin became General Secretary of the
Communist party in Russia.
Civil war between factions in the Irish Free
State. Michael Collins, chairman of Irish
Provisional Government, killed.
Lloyd George lost his position as Prime
Minister.

◀ The Earl and Countess of
Strathmore, George V and Queen
Mary with their son and daughter in
law the Duke and Duchess of York at
the christening of their daughter
Elizabeth, now Elizabeth II.

1923

Conservatives won general election,
Labour gained more seats than Liberals.
Bonar Law became Conservative Prime
Minister. He was soon replaced by Stanley
Baldwin.
In Germany, Hitler was imprisoned after a
Nazi uprising in Munich failed. German
currency collapsed. Before the war, £1
sterling bought 24 German marks. By
23 November 1923, £1 was worth 95 million
marks, and a week later, 18½ *billion* marks.
In sport, the Le Mans 24-hour motor race,
and the F.A. Cup Final at Wembley were
held for the first time.

1924

Labour-Liberal coalition with Ramsay
MacDonald (Labour) as Prime Minister.
Policies included increasing unemployment
benefit, agricultural wages and council
house subsidies, and helping to finance
Imperial Airways. In October, the
Conservatives won the General Election
and took power again.
British Empire Exhibition at Wembley.

1925

Enquiry held into coal miners' dispute, and
temporary settlement made. (Samuel
Commission).
Hitler published 'Mein Kampf' Vol. 1.
First transatlantic broadcast.
Pneumatic tyres first used on London
buses.
Work began on the Mersey tunnel (opened
1934).

1926

Miners went on strike, May 1st to November
19th.
General strike in Britain, May 4th-12th.
John Logie Baird first demonstrated
television.
The Central Electricity Board was set up to
carry power over long distances and build
the National Grid.
Germany was admitted to the League of
Nations.
On 21 April, a daughter was born to the
Duke and Duchess of York. She was to
become Queen Elizabeth II.

Index

This index will help you to find some of the important things in *How We Used to Live*. The page numbers shown in **dark letters** refer to illustrations. The dates, *in italics*, show you where to look in the 'Important Events' section on pages 46-47.